John White's Lost Colony

by Kiyomi Hirigashi
illustrated by Gina Capaldi

Harcourt
SCHOOL PUBLISHERS

Printed in China

ISBN 10: 0-15-351544-9
ISBN 13: 978-0-15-351544-6

Ordering Options
ISBN 10: 0-15-351214-8 (Grade 4 Advanced Collection)
ISBN 13: 978-0-15-351214-8 (Grade 4 Advanced Collection)
ISBN 10: 0-15-358134-4 (package of 5)
ISBN 13: 978-0-15-358134-2 (package of 5)

5 6 7 8 9 10 985 12 11 10 09

John White glared at Christopher Newport, the captain of the ship called *Hopewell*, as the crew snickered. White had been complaining to Captain Newport that the crew was spoiled and coddled. The crew, used to his outbursts, continued to eat. Captain Newport, too, was not bothered by White's complaints.

"Mr. White," Newport said calmly, "you knew full well when you came aboard my ship that the voyage had not one, but *two* goals."

"Yes, Captain, and the first goal has been attained, sir! We have gathered riches for England, and the ship is now filled with ginger and silver and hides!" Captain Newport smiled, pleased with the ship's impressive cargo.

"Now," White continued, "it is time to meet our second goal—to sail to Roanoke!"

"Tomorrow," replied the captain, pausing to take a dainty little bite of food, "we shall sail toward Hispaniola." White stormed off.

John White had good reason to be upset: he was worried about his people. Three years earlier, in 1587, White had sailed from England to North America to start a new colony there. About 150 colonists had joined him. They landed on Roanoke Island off the coast of Virginia in late July. The ship was anchored offshore as the colonists unloaded the supplies. The ship along with White would sail back to England once the colonists were settled.

White soon realized that the colonists would need far more supplies than they had. The colonists asked White to sail back to England and get what they needed. White would obtain a wide variety of supplies, and then he would sail back to Roanoke.

Before his departure, White told the colonists to leave him a message if they moved. "Carve words into a tree someplace where I will see it. If you have to leave because you're in danger, carve a cross above the words."

White sailed home and found England at war with Spain. Spain had a huge fleet of ships called the Armada. The English ordered all ships to be used against the Armada. Therefore, there was no ship for White to use to return to the colony.

Finally, White found a group of ships that were being allowed to sail to the West Indies, near North America, to look for treasure. Then the ships would take White back to Roanoke Island. On March 20, 1590, the *Hopewell* and several other ships departed from England. White was determined to get back to his colony.

For months, the ships made a memorable
journey around the West Indies. At last, on August
12, the ships reached Roanoke. Because the water
near the island was shallow, the ships had to
anchor three miles (4.83 km) away. White and the
crew boarded two small boats in order to row to
Roanoke. On the way, they saw smoke coming
from nearby Hatarask Island. "That must be their
signal fire. We must go there," White said.

They rowed to Hatarask and walked along
the sandy beach for hours. It was hot, and the
crew muttered complaints. White, though, was a
dedicated man, and he was absolutely determined
to find the colonists. Unfortunately, there was no
sign of any people. The fire must have started
naturally. "Let's rest now and row to Roanoke
tomorrow," White decided.

The next morning, they were ready to row to Roanoke, although the wind was blowing hard and the waves grew taller and stronger. It would be an extremely dangerous crossing. The crew struggled to row the two small boats out to sea against the high waves.

White's boat filled with water, but the other boat actually turned over. The six men on the boat toppled into the churning sea, and there was no way to save them. They all drowned. The remaining crewmembers were stunned and didn't think they could endure any more hardship, but White persuaded them to keep rowing.

It was already dark by the time they arrived near where the colony stood. "Look, I see a light," White said. They rowed toward it and saw a large fire burning. "That must be them!" White yelled happily. They could not risk rowing to shore in the dark, so they anchored the boats.

"They might think we're waiting to attack them and fire upon us," said a crewmember. White agreed and decided to let the colonists know that he and his crew were not a threat.

"HELLO, GOOD ENGLISH MATES!" White yelled. There was no response from the island, so White turned to Nelson, a crewmember, and said, "Play your trumpet to ease their fears." Nelson played, but again the island was silent.

White and the men slept in the boats that night. In the morning, they rowed ashore to Roanoke. They walked toward the area where they had seen the fire the night before. White was disappointed to see a large patch of burnt grass and a smoking rotten tree. "Another fire made by nature, not humans," White said. "Nonetheless, we must press on," he added.

The Roanoke colonists had built a small village on the northern part of the island, so White assumed that's where the colonists were. He was confident that he would find the colonists one way or another. White and the men left the woods and walked for a long time along the Roanoke shoreline. He then led the crew up a sand dune toward where the village had been.

At the top of the dune, White noticed a tree that had a slash in it, so he walked up to take a closer look. "Now *there* is a good sign," said White as he pointed to the trunk of the tree, which clearly had the letters *CRO* carved into it.

"*CRO*?" Captain Newport asked, confused.

"Yes, *CRO*," answered White. "Before I left, I instructed the colonists to leave me a message if they had to leave the island for any reason. This must be their message."

"Yet, these are merely letters that do not even spell a word—how can you be so sure?" Newport asked.

"Obviously, these are Roman letters which would have only been carved by a person from Europe, not by a person from North America," White explained.

When they reached the site of the village, White noticed that the word *CROATOAN* was carved into one of the fence posts. "They have left me a message telling me where they've gone! They're on Croatoan, which is an island not far from here," he explained.

Captain Newport laughed, and he said, "That is pitiful. It is merely what you *wish* to believe, Mr. White. You have no proof that the colonists made it to Croatoan. They easily could have gone somewhere else, or they could have been picked up by a ship. Worse, they could have been attacked by the local people."

"No, Captain, you are wrong," said White. "You see, the colonists were also told to carve a cross above their message if they were in danger. As you can see, there is no such cross."

In the village, White and the men saw that the wooden houses the colonists had built were now taken apart. "The colonists were probably attacked, and the village was destroyed," Captain Newport said.

"Maybe the colonists simply took the things they needed, such as wood, when they left for Croatoan," White said.

"Then why would they leave this kettle?" Newport asked, pointing to a large iron cooking pot on the ground.

"Perhaps it was too heavy for them to take on the boat," White replied. Beyond the kettle a ways, they saw a rifle.

"I suppose they didn't need this rifle?" asked Newport skeptically.

White didn't want to believe that anything bad had happened to the colonists. "Perhaps the rifle being left behind is just a fluke. Maybe they just forgot it when they left," he replied.

"Well, I do hope the colonists are safe at Croatoan," said Captain Newport. "We shall sail there tomorrow and hope to find them. Now, however, the skies are looking stormy, and I believe we need to get back to the ship before nightfall."

White and the others agreed. Before leaving the village, White turned and took one last look around. He wondered what would have happened if only he had been able to come back sooner with supplies. Then he said to himself, *"Perhaps Croatoan is an even better place for my colony. I shall see tomorrow."*

That night, a horrible storm tossed the ship around. Captain Newport feared that the anchor would break loose, and the ship would be at the mercy of the dangerous waves. Fortunately, though, it held, and they survived the night.

The next morning, Captain Newport tried to guide the ship to Croatoan, but the continuing bad weather prevented him. The ship was low on food and water, so Newport suggested that they sail back to the West Indies for the winter, stock up on supplies, and return to Croatoan in the spring.

As the ship sailed south, more bad weather pushed it farther off course. Finally, Captain Newport decided that the only safe move would be to sail the ship back to England, which he did.

John White was disappointed. This would be his last attempt to find the colonists. In the remaining years of his life, he called for others to search for the colonists, but they were never found. Today, White's colony is referred to as the legendary "lost colony."

Think Critically

1. How does John White feel about the missing colonists?

2. What happened just before White and the crew were about to row to Roanoke Island for the first time?

3. Explain what the phrase "lost colony" means.

4. Why did John White ask Nelson to play his trumpet?

5. What do you think happened to the colonists?

Social Studies

Find Out More There are many locations mentioned in this book, such as England, the West Indies, and Roanoke island. Choose one and find out five facts about it.

School-Home Connection Discuss John White's "lost colony" with family members. Invite them to share what they think happened to the colonists.